# PACIFIC ISLANDS
## COOK BOOK

RECIPES BY
**MONICA BAYLEY**
ILLUSTRATIONS BY
**BRUCE BUTTE**

Pacific Islands Cook Book
© 1977 by Determined Productions, Inc.
World Rights Reserved

Published by
Determined Productions, Inc.
Box 2150
San Francisco
California, 94126

Library of Congress Catalogue Card No. 77-78296
ISBN No. 0-915696-05-3

Printed in the United States of America

# TABLE OF CONTENTS

# ISLAND FEASTS

The cooking of the Pacific islands reflects the influence of many Asiatic and European culinary styles. Authentic local recipes are combined with those brought to the islands by settlers and travelers of many races and national origins, resulting in a delightful variety of uses of tropical fruits, vegetables and seafood. Those who came were colonialists, adventurers, imported laborers, traders and settlers — British, French, Spanish, Chinese, Yankee, Japanese, Korean — each culture left its mark. The history of the Pacific can be read in island food.

You can turn a meal into an island feast, brighten your table with a single exotic dish or treat your friends to an authentic feast from one of these islands in the sun. The author traveled extensively throughout the Pacific islands to collect these tempting tropical recipes. Each has been tested to assure happy results and Bruce Butte has seasoned the book with his delightful drawings.

Feasts in the Pacific islands are usually preceded by traditional drinking ceremonies which vary from island to island but are all designed to make visitors and guests feel honored and welcome. The usual appetizer is some kind of raw fish marinated in lemon or lime juice. Suckling pigs, roasts of meat, whole fowls, fish, shellfish and vegetables are wrapped in leaves, then roasted and steamed over hot stones in underground ovens until tender. Feasts are topped off with puddings, pies or cakes and always include a variety of fresh fruits. An evening of singing and dancing follows.

# MENUS

Most feast dishes can be adapted for preparation in modern ovens and substitutions such as the following can be made: corn husks or foil for ti leaves, fresh spinach leaves for taro leaves, coarse kosher salt for Hawaiian red salt, pork roasts for suckling pig.

## HAWAIIAN LUAU
Mai Tais
Lomi Lomi Salmon or Sashimi
Luau Pork Roast
Chicken Luau or Chicken with Long Rice
Lau Laus (made with pork, fish and spinach)
Roasted Sweet Potatoes or Yams
Pineapple and Bananas
Hawaiian Haupia

## TAHITIAN TAMAARAA
Tahitian Punch
Poisson Crû
Roasted Chicken with Stuffing
Samoan Snapper
Steamed Lobster or Crayfish
Roasted Sweet Potatoes
Tahitian Pies

## FIJIAN MAGITI
Fiji Fizzes
Ika Lolo (Poisson Crû)
Beef Tartare
Barbecued Pork

Pineapple Chicken
Steamed Crabs or Prawns
Roasted Yams
Coconut Cake
Mangoes and Papayas

## TONGAN FEAST
Tonga Punch
Tonga Eggs
Cold Fish Fillets
Pineapple Pork Chops
Roasted Chicken
Lau Laus (made with corned beef)
Roasted Cassava or Yams
Tonga Pie or Melanesian Macaroons

## PHILIPPINE MABUHAY FEAST
Beer
Lumpia
Escabeche
Philippine Beef Soup
Pancit or Sotanghon
Pork Adobo
Lime Leche Flan

## GUAMANIAN CHAMORRO FEAST
Beer
Lumpia with Guamanian Hot Sauce
Shrimp Kelaguen
Guamanian Potato Salad
Chamorro Spareribs
Spanish Rice
Lime Pie

# A NOTE ABOUT CHILIES

Many of the recipes in this book call for fresh green chili peppers or ground red peppers. Be careful in selecting and preparing them, for there are many kinds of chilies which vary in size, color and degree of hotness. The amounts in these recipes are calculated for medium-hot dishes. They may be increased or decreased to suit your taste.

## GREEN CHILI PEPPERS

When recipes call for green chili peppers, use the mild 6-inch long California or Anaheim chilies, fresh or canned. When recipes call for *hot* green chili peppers, use medium-size 2 to 3-inch long Jalapenos, fresh or canned.

## PREPARATION

Wash under cold water, break off stems. Using a small sharp knife, scrape out seeds and veins and rinse. Cut in half and lay skin side down on chopping board. Slice or chop very carefully and when you finish, wash your hands, the knife and the board in soapy water. Do not touch your face with your hands while preparing chili peppers.

## RED PEPPERS

Crushed, dried red chili peppers and ground red peppers are available in most stores where spices are sold. When recipes in this book call for dried red peppers use the small half-inch long dry red peppers and crush carefully in a mortar. Other recipes will specify ground red peppers or cayenne.

# A NOTE ABOUT COCONUT MILK & CREAM

## COCONUT MILK

1 fresh coconut, or 1 (7-oz.) package or can of flaked coconut

Pierce eyes of fresh coconut and drain liquid. Crack shell and remove meat. Peel meat and cut into inch-square pieces.

Made *with a blender:* Put ½ cup meat in blender. Add 1 cup hot water. Blend 30 seconds. Pour out into strainer lined with cheesecloth over deep bowl. Squeeze and press coconut against strainer to extract milk. Discard pressed meat. Repeat this process 3 more times. Makes about 4 cups.

Made *without a blender:* Put a quart-size strainer lined with cheesecloth into a bowl just big enough for the strainer to fit into. Put 4 cups freshly grated coconut into strainer. Pour 2 cups boiling water over the coconut. Let stand ½ hour. If using packaged or canned coconut, let stand 1½ hours. Squeeze and press coconut against strainer to extract milk. Makes about 2 cups. Process can be repeated twice more using same coconut but adding only 1 cup boiling water each time.

## COCONUT CREAM

Prepare coconut milk. Let stand for an hour or more until cream rises to top. Skim cream and use as directed. 4 cups milk make about 1½ cups cream.

# APPETIZERS AND FIRST COURSES
(ALLOW ⅛ POUND PER SERVING OF RAW FISH APPETIZERS)

# LOMI LOMI SALMON
(LOMI MEANS TO PRESS OR SQUEEZE)

½ pound fresh or salted salmon
    *Fresh* salmon: Remove skin and bones. Shred. Put in glass or ceramic
      bowl with 1 teaspoon salt and juice of 2 lemons or limes. Marinate 6
      hours in refrigerator. Drain.
    *Salted* salmon: Soak in warm water 6 hours. Drain. Remove skin and
      bones. Shred.
2 large ripe tomatoes, peeled, chopped
4 scallions, minced
2 or 3 dashes Tabasco sauce
½ cup crushed ice
    Shredded lettuce or watercress

Prepare salmon. Put in glass or ceramic bowl. Add tomatoes, scallions and
Tabasco. Press or squeeze with hands until thoroughly mixed. Cover and
chill for 1 hour. Just before serving add crushed ice and mix. Serve small
portions on beds of shredded lettuce or watercress.

6

# POISSON CRÛ
(TAHITIAN RAW FISH OR FIJIAN IKA LOLO)

½ pound absolutely fresh raw fish (firm salt-water fish such as tuna, halibut, snapper or swordfish)
½ teaspoon coarse salt
  Juice of 3 limes or lemons
2 tablespoons chopped scallions
½ clove garlic, minced
1 cup coconut milk (page 5)
  Shredded lettuce

Remove skin, bones and any dark portions of fish. Lay fish on cutting board and cut across the grain into ⅛-inch-thick slices. Put in bowl. Sprinkle with salt and lime juice. Cover and let stand in refrigerator 4 to 5 hours. Drain juice. Add garlic and scallions and mix well. Add coconut milk. Refrigerate for 1 hour before serving. Serve small individual portions on beds of shredded lettuce.

# SASHIMI
(JAPANESE RAW FISH)

¾ pound absolutely fresh red tuna, swordfish, halibut or bonito
½ cup soy sauce
3 tablespoons water
1 teaspoon sugar
3 tablespoons wasabi powder (Japanese horseradish) or hot dry
    mustard made into a thick paste with small amount of water
2 cups grated fresh peeled Chinese turnips, Japanese daikon or white
    icicle radishes

Remove skin, bones and any dark portions of fish. Cut across the grain into
⅛-inch-thick slices about 2 inches long. Mix soy sauce, water and sugar in
cup. Mix horseradish paste and let stand in covered bowl for 5 minutes. Serve
individual portions by placing ½ teaspoon of paste, small dish of soy sauce
mixture, ½ dozen slices of fish and small mound of grated turnip on each
plate. To eat: Mix paste with soy sauce and dip slices of fish in mixture. Alternate bites of fish and turnip.

# ESCABECHE

## (PHILIPPINE FRIED PICKLED FISH)

1½ pounds fresh snapper or sea bass fillets
1 teaspoon salt
  Flour
¼ cup cooking oil
1 onion, peeled, seeded, minced
½ green chili pepper, peeled, minced
1 clove garlic, peeled, minced
1 cup water
1 tablespoon corn starch
1 tablespoon malt vinegar
1 tablespoon sugar
2 tablespoons soy sauce
1 teaspoon minced fresh ginger root

Sprinkle fish with salt and roll it in flour. Heat oil in frying pan until hot. Fry fillets until brown on both sides, then remove from pan. Add onion, chili, and garlic and sauté until onion is golden. Mix water, cornstarch, vinegar, sugar, and soy sauce and add. Add ginger root. Stir well. Bring to a boil while stirring. Lay fillets on sauce. Cover and cook gently for about 5 minutes or until fish flakes easily when tested with a fork. Serve with boiled rice and vegetables.

# PRAWN ANEMONES

½ pound fresh prawns or shrimp, cleaned, deveined, minced
2 tablespoons minced scallions
6 canned water chestnuts, minced
1 tablespoon sherry
1 teaspoon salt
2 teaspoons cornstarch
1 cup Chinese rice sticks (Py Mei Fun), crushed
  Oil for deep-frying

Combine all ingredients except rice sticks. Shape into a dozen balls. Crush rice sticks on pastry cloth with rolling pin. Roll balls in crushed sticks, pressing until they are covered. Heat oil to deep-fry temperature (375°). Deep-fry balls a few at a time until lightly browned and sticks have puffed up and turned crisp.

# SHRIMP KELAGUEN

2 cups minced cooked shrimp
½ cup fresh grated coconut
¼ cup lime juice
2 tablespoons minced onion
1 hot green chili pepper, minced fine

Combine all ingredients in a bowl, mix thoroughly, let stand an hour before serving. Serve in a mound on a salad plate with small cherry tomatoes and celery sticks.

# SEAFOOD TURNOVERS

2 dozen won ton skins or wrappers (ready-made fresh or frozen dough squares available in most large grocery stores). Thaw frozen ones in refrigerator before using. Or make your own as follows:

SKINS
  2 cups flour
  1 teaspoon salt
  1 egg, beaten
1/3 cup ice water

Sift flour and salt together into deep bowl. Add egg and mix. Add water a few drops at a time while blending and stirring with a fork until dough is formed. Turn out on floured pastry board. Knead for a few minutes until smooth. Chill. Roll out paper-thin. Cut circles of dough with 2½-inch cookie cutter or glass rim. Cover with damp cloth to keep from drying out until filled.

Fillings: (Make one of these, mixing ingredients in order given. Leftover filling can be frozen for later use.)

FILLING 1
  1 package (8-oz.) cream cheese
  1 cup minced cooked crab meat or shrimp
  ¼ cup soft bread crumbs
  ¼ teaspoon sesame oil
  ½ teaspoon salt
  ¼ teaspoon pepper
  2 teaspoons lemon juice

## FILLING 2

1/4 pound ground pork, sautéed for 5 minutes
1/4 pound prawns, boiled, deveined, minced
6 shrimp, boiled, deveined, minced
1/2 cup minced water chestnuts
1 tablespoon soy sauce
1/2 teaspoon salt
1 egg, beaten
1/2 cup minced scallions
   Oil for deep-frying
   Hot mustard and catsup for dipping

Put skins on pastry board a few at a time. If using ready-made ones, make circles by putting a glass rim the same diameter as the squares on each square and running a sharp knife blade around outside of rim. Put a teaspoonful of filling on each circle. Fold over into half-moon shape and crimp edges together with fork tines, pressing down hard all along the edge to make a tight seal. If edges get too dry, moisten lower edge with a drop of water on fingertip before sealing. Heat oil in deep, heavy skillet to 375°. Fry turnovers 4 or 5 at a time, turning once (takes 3 or 4 minutes), until golden on both sides. Remove with slotted spoon. Drain on absorbent paper. Put on cookie sheets in warm oven until ready to serve. Serve with small bowls of mustard and catsup for dipping.

# COLD FISH FILLETS
(WITH SAUCE VINAIGRETTE)

1½ pounds fresh white large-boned fish (cod, haddock or snapper) fillets
   1 quart court bouillon (page 52)
   1 cup sauce vinaigrette (page 82)

Cut fillets into 4-inch-square portions. Poach gently in simmering court bouillon 5 to 10 minutes or until just tender. Remove carefully with slotted spoon and place in shallow dish. Pour sauce vinaigrette over fish. Turn carefully to coat both sides with sauce. Chill thoroughly. Serve one portion per person.

# ISLE OF PINES PRAWNS

   1 dozen large prawns or jumbo shrimp (2 per serving)
   1 quart court bouillon (page 52)
   2 dry onions, peeled and shredded
   3 carrots, peeled and shredded
   2 cups coconut milk (page 5)
     Salt to taste
   3 hard-cooked eggs, crumbled

Peel prawns and devein. Simmer in court bouillon about 10 minutes or until pink and tender. Remove with slotted spoon. Cool. Chop. Mix with shredded onions and carrots. Add coconut milk. Salt to taste. Serve in large clam or scallop shells, or island-style in scooped out half coconut shells. Top with crumbled egg.

14

# CLAM ROLLS

8 (6-inch-square) egg roll skins (ready-made fresh or frozen noodle-like
   dough squares available in most large grocery stores). Thaw frozen
   ones in refrigerator before using. Or, make your own using recipe
   for skins for Seafood Turnovers (page 12), cutting dough into
   6-inch-squares.
Oil for frying

FILLING:
3 (7½-oz.) cans minced clams, drained
1 (8-oz.) package cream cheese
4 Holland rusks, crushed
1 dozen ripe olives, minced
1 teaspoon Worcestershire sauce
3 tablespoons minced scallions
½ teaspoon pepper

Mix all filling ingredients in order given. Lay skins on lightly-floured pastry
board. Put a mound of filling in center of each one. Spread filling flat to within
½ inch of each edge. With pastry brush dipped in water moisten one edge.
Roll opposite edge up to moistened edge and press firmly to seal the roll.
Tuck in roll ends securely. Heat about 2 inches of oil in large skillet to deep-
fry temperature (375°). Fry two at a time until golden on all sides. Remove
with slotted spoon. Drain on absorbent paper. Serve on platter with each roll
cut diagonally into 4 slices. Serve with mustard and catsup.

# BEEF BALLS
(KOREAN STYLE)

  1 pound lean ground beef
  2 tablespoons soy sauce
  ¼ teaspoon sesame oil
  2 teaspoons peanut oil
  2 teaspoons sugar
  1 tablespoon minced scallions
  ½ clove garlic, minced
  ¼ teaspoon salt
  4 dried mushrooms, soaked in water ½ hour, drained, chopped
    Flour for dredging
  1 egg, beaten
    Oil for frying

Combine all ingredients except flour and egg and mix thoroughly. Shape into 2 dozen small balls. Roll balls in flour. Dip in beaten egg. Fry in hot skillet in 2 or 3 tablespoons oil, turning to brown on all sides. Drain on absorbent paper. Serve hot.

# PIPIKAULA
(JERKED BEEF)

  1 pound flank steak, chilled in freezer for 15 minutes, cut with grain into ⅛-inch-thick slices. Marinate overnight in 1/3 cup soy sauce, ¼ cup sherry, ½ cup sugar, 1 clove peeled, minced garlic, and 1 teaspoon grated fresh ginger root.

Remove strips of steak from marinade. Lay on upper oven rack across grids. Put foil on lower rack to catch drips. Bake 165° for 3 hours or more, until very dry. Take out. Cut into 4-inch lengths. Can be made ahead and stored in tightly closed glass jar until used.

# BEEF TARTARE
(NEW CALEDONIA STYLE)

1 pound lean ground raw beef (sirloin or top round steak)
2 tablespoons light soy sauce
2 teaspoons sugar
½ teaspoon sesame seed oil
1 teaspoon salad oil
½ teaspoon salt
¼ teaspoon pepper
½ clove garlic, minced
1 teaspoon sesame seeds, toasted (page 54)
1 tablespoon chopped scallions
　Pear, mango and melon slices

Put all ingredients except beef and fruit slices into a jar. Put lid on tight and shake hard to mix. Add to steak and mix thoroughly. Form into smooth mound and place in center of platter. Encircle with thin slices of peeled pears, mangoes, and melon. Serve with thin slices of French or rye bread.

# CORNED BEEF CANAPES

(MOOREAN)

1 can (12 oz.) corned beef, thoroughly chilled, cut into
    ¼-inch-thick slices
2 scallions, minced
1 large fresh tomato, sliced
2 tablespoons vinegar
4 tablespoons olive oil
    Salt and pepper to taste
    Thin slices of French or dark rye bread

Put corned beef slices in shallow dish. Add scallions and tomato slices. Mix vinegar and oil and pour over slices. Add salt and pepper. Let stand 5 minutes. Turn slices over gently to coat with dressing. Cut small slices of beef and tomato and make tiny open-faced sandwiches.

# STUFFED SNOW PEAS

3 dozen Chinese snow peas
    Boiling water for blanching
4 ounces cream cheese, seasoned to taste with salt, pepper and
    Worcestershire sauce

Take strings off pea pods. Cover with boiling water. Let stand 5 minutes. Drain. Mash cheese and add seasonings. Split pea pods with knife blade. Stuff with cheese and pinch halves back together. Chill.

# RUMAKI
## (CHICKEN LIVERS, WATER CHESTNUTS & BACON)

1 clove garlic, peeled, minced
1 inch-long piece of fresh ginger
    root, peeled, minced
1 tablespoon star anise
2 cups soy sauce
1 cup chicken broth
1 pound fresh chicken livers
1 can (5-oz.) whole water chestnuts
½ pound thinly sliced bacon
    Peanut oil for deep frying

Put soy sauce and broth into a saucepan. Add garlic, ginger root and anise. Bring to a boil, turn heat down and simmer for 4 to 5 minutes. Add chicken livers, simmer for 10 minutes, remove with slotted spoon and spread out to cool. Cut water chestnuts and bacon slices into thirds. Wrap a piece of bacon around one piece each of water chestnut and chicken liver. Secure with a toothpick. When all the rumakis are finished, heat oil to deep fry temperature and drop them, a few at a time into the hot oil. Fry until bacon is brown and crisp. Serve immediately.

# TONGA EGGS

6 hard-cooked eggs, peeled and cut in half
3 tablespoons coconut milk (page 5)
2 tablespoons prepared horseradish
    Salt and pepper to taste
    Sliced olives for topping

Remove egg yolks and mash fine. Add coconut milk, horseradish, salt and pepper. Fill egg-white halves with yolk mixture and top with sliced olives.

19

# LUMPIA

## (DEEP-FRIED CHICKEN, PORK & VEGETABLE ROLLS)

WRAPPERS:
1¼ cups instant all-purpose flour
1¼ cups cold water
    Oil for cooking

Mix flour and water and beat to a thin paste consistency. Put an 8-inch frying pan over medium heat. Dip a pastry brush into oil and brush the bottom of the pan lightly. Take a 2-inch-wide paint brush and dip it into the paste. Using a full brush and working fast, paint the bottom of the pan with a thin even sheet of paste. Cook for a few seconds until the edges of the wrapper start to curl. Lift out and lay on waxed, floured paper. Oil the pan lightly and repeat the process until the paste is used. Makes a dozen wrappers.

FILLING:
  1 large chicken breast
  1 pound lean, boneless pork,
    cubed
  1 small onion, peeled, cut in half
1½ teaspoons salt
  1 bay leaf
    Water
  2 tablespoons peanut oil
  1 teaspoon minced garlic

½ cup minced scallions
½ green chili pepper, seeded, minced
2 cups finely shredded cabbage
1 cup slivered green beans
1 cup finely chopped carrots
1 cup finely chopped celery
2 tablespoons soy sauce
3 cups peanut oil for deep frying

Put chicken, pork, onion, salt, and bay leaf into a saucepan. Add water to cover. Bring to a boil, then turn down heat and simmer covered until chicken

20

and pork are just tender. Remove chicken and pork, strain broth and reserve. When chicken and pork are cool enough to handle, skin and bone the chicken, then chop chicken and pork coarsely. Put the 2 tablespoons of oil into a large frying pan. Sauté garlic, scallions, and chili for a minute or two, add chicken and pork and brown slightly. Add cabbage, beans, carrots, and celery and stir. Add the soy sauce to 1 cup of reserved broth and add. Stir and cook for 4 or 5 minutes. Empty mixture into a colander and let it drain thoroughly.

Put about half a cup of the cooked mixture in the center of a wrapper. Shape it into a roll, leaving an inch of space at each end. Fold one side of the wrapper over the roll, fold the two ends over that, then fold the other side of the wrapper over them. Press last flap down securely. Repeat this procedure until all the wrappers are filled. Heat oil in deep fryer to 375°. Using a slotted spoon, drop the lumpias, a few at a time, into the hot oil and deep fry until golden brown and crisp. Serve with one of the following dipping sauces.

## PHILIPPINE VINEGAR SAUCE
1½ tablespoons peeled, minced garlic
1½ teaspoons salt
1½ cups malt vinegar

Crush garlic and salt in a mortar to make a paste. Add vinegar. Beat with a fork to mix thoroughly. Give each diner a dipping bowl with about ¼ cup of sauce.

## GUAMANIAN HOT SAUCE
 8 tablespoons soy sauce
 2 tablespoons fresh lemon juice
 2 tablespoons vinegar
 1 teaspoon minced hot chili peppers
 1 teaspoon minced scallions

# CHINESE MEATBALL SOUP

2 quarts water

MEATBALLS:
1 pound ground beef (chuck)
1 egg
1 tablespoon cornstarch
7 tablespoons soy sauce
½ dry onion, minced
½ teaspoon salt
¼ teaspoon pepper

Mix all ingredients together thoroughly, then shape into 1-inch-wide balls.

4 cups shredded Chinese celery cabbage
1 cup shredded carrots

Put water in soup pot and bring to a boil. Drop meatballs into pot, a few at a time, until they are all in the pot. Simmer uncovered 10 minutes. Add celery cabbage and carrots and simmer until vegetables are just tender.

# ISLAND FISH CHOWDER

¼ pound salt pork, cut into thin 1-inch-long strips
2 tablespoons peanut oil
1 large onion, sliced
6 firm potatoes, peeled and diced
1 pound cod or haddock, fresh or frozen, boned and cut into
    bite-size pieces
2 cups water
3 fresh tomatoes, peeled and chopped
3 cups half-and-half, or 1½ cups each milk and cream
    Salt and pepper to taste

Put oil in deep, heavy stew pot. Sauté pork pieces until brown. Remove bits of pork with slotted spoon and set aside. Sauté onion slices until yellow. Add potatoes and saute for a few minutes. Add 1 cup water and simmer until just tender. Add tomatoes. Put fish in saucepan with 1 cup water. Simmer until tender. Drain. Cool. Flake. Add to potato mixture. Add milk and bring to a boil. Turn flame down low and simmer for a few minutes. Add salt and pepper. Serve piping hot.

# RED SNAPPER SOUP

    2 pounds red snapper, boned, cut into 2-inch-wide slices
    1 onion, sliced
    1 leek, chopped (use white part only)
    1 cup diced potatoes
    1 teaspoon salt
    ½ teaspoon pepper, freshly ground
    1 cup sherry
    1 quart water
       Juice of ½ lemon or lime

Put onions, leek and potatoes in soup pot. Add salt and pepper. Lay fish slices on top. Add water, sherry and lemon juice. Simmer covered until vegetables and fish are tender. Serve hot.

# PHILIPPINE BEEF SOUP

1½ tablespoons cooking oil
1 clove garlic, peeled, minced
1 teaspoon minced fresh ginger root
2 onions, peeled, chopped
½ pound lean ground beef
1 large fresh tomato, peeled, chopped
1 quart water
4 beef bouillon cubes
2 teaspoons salt
½ teaspoon pepper
3 celery cabbage leaves, chopped

Heat oil in stew pot. Add garlic, ginger, and onions. Sauté until onions are golden. Add beef and stir and fry until brown. Add tomato, water, bouillon cubes, salt and pepper. Simmer 15 minutes. Add celery cabbage and simmer another 5 minutes.

# OYSTER BISQUE

1 quart oysters
1 tablespoon butter
1 tablespoon flour
1 quart half-and-half, scalded
½ cup minced celery
1 green pepper, seeded, minced fine
   Salt and pepper to taste
   Pinch of cayenne pepper
   Dash Worcestershire sauce

Put oysters, liquid included, through a grinder or put into a blender for 20 seconds to chop fine. Set aside. Make a thin cream sauce by melting the butter, adding the flour and mixing well, then adding scalded milk gradually, stirring constantly until mixture comes to a boil. Add the celery, green pepper, salt, pepper and cayenne. Add the oysters and heat until hot but do not boil. Add Worcestershire sauce and serve immediately.

# POLYNESIAN ROAST DUCK
(WITH COCONUT-CURRY SAUCE)

    1 (4 to 5 pound) domestic duck (allow 1 pound per serving)
    2 tablespoons flour
    4 tablespoons butter or margarine
    1 cup water
    1 fresh pineapple, peeled, cored, cut into chunks
        or 3 cups frozen or canned pineapple chunks
    1 fresh papaya, peeled, seeded, sliced
        or 2 cups canned chunks

COCONUT-CURRY SAUCE:
    1 quart coconut milk (page 5). Prepare and set aside for 1 hour to
        allow cream to rise.
    2 tablespoons butter or margarine
    1 clove garlic, minced
    2 medium-size onions, chopped
    An inch-square cube fresh ginger root, peeled and grated
        or ½ teaspoon ground ginger
    1 tablespoon curry powder
    4 tablespoons flour
    1 teaspoon salt

Skim cream from coconut milk and set aside. Melt butter in saucepan. Add garlic, onions and ginger and sauté until onions are yellow and tender. Add curry powder, flour and salt. Stir well. Add coconut milk, stirring constantly. Cook 15 minutes stirring every few minutes. Remove from fire. Put through food mill or sieve. Return to saucepan. Add coconut cream and heat being careful not to let mixture boil.

Cut off leg, thigh pieces and breast meat from duck and trim excess fat. Flour lightly. Put butter in heavy skillet. Sauté duck pieces until brown. Add 1 cup water. Simmer covered for an hour or until tender. Put drained pineapple and papaya chunks in shallow baking dish. Lay duck pieces on top. Cover with sauce. Bake 350° oven 15 minutes.

# CHICKEN LUAU

2 frying chickens, cut into serving pieces
2 tablespoons butter
2 tablespoons margarine
2 teaspoons salt
1 teaspoon pepper
2 cups chicken broth
3 pounds fresh spinach
3 cups coconut milk (page 5)

Put butter and margarine in stew pot and sauté chicken pieces until brown. Add salt, pepper and broth. Simmer covered until tender. Remove chicken pieces to deep serving dish and set aside in warm oven. Wash spinach. Break or nip off stems. Cook, with only water remaining on leaves from washing, until just tender. Drain. Cut coarsely with knife blade. Add coconut milk to chicken broth and heat to boiling point. Add spinach and stir gently. Pour over chicken and serve. (6 servings).

# CHICKEN WITH LONG RICE

6 ounces Chinese rice noodles prepared as on page 87
2 frying chickens, cut into serving pieces
  Water to cover
2 tablespoons butter
2 tablespoons margarine
1 stalk celery, chopped
1 (1½-inch-square) cube fresh ginger root, peeled and grated
  or ¾ teaspoon ground ginger
2 teaspoons salt
½ teaspoon pepper
3 scallions, chopped
2 tablespoons soy sauce

Prepare long rice and set aside. Put butter and margarine in stew pot and sauté chicken until brown. Add water to cover. Add celery, ginger, salt and pepper. Simmer covered until tender. Remove chicken pieces and put in warm oven. Add scallions and soy sauce to broth. Simmer 10 minutes. Add chicken pieces and long rice. Simmer covered 5 minutes. (6 servings.)

# PINEAPPLE CHICKEN

4 chicken breasts, split and skinned (allow ½ breast per serving)
¼ cup margarine or butter
½ cup flour
1¼ cups chicken broth
1 cup half-and-half or light cream
1 teaspoon salt
½ teaspoon pepper
1 teaspoon grated lemon peel
3 tablespoons sherry
8 rings of fresh or canned pineapple
1 can (4-oz.) pimentos, seeded
½ cup slivered almonds, toasted

Melt margarine in heavy pan. Add flour and stir until smooth. Add chicken broth and milk slowly, stirring until thickened. Add salt, pepper, lemon peel and sherry. Put chicken pieces in sauce. Cover and simmer for ½ hour. When tender, top with pineapple rings and pimentos. Cover and heat until hot. Sprinkle with almonds.

# ISLAND STUFFING
(FOR CHICKEN OR TURKEY)

4 cups bread cubes or crumbs (day-old bread is best)
3 tablespoons butter
3 tablespoons oil
½ cup chopped onions
½ cup chopped celery
½ cup chopped macadamia nuts
1 cup chopped green apples
6 Chinese mushrooms, soaked in water ½ hour, drained, chopped

Combine butter and oil in heavy skillet and sauté bread cubes for 5 minutes, stirring constantly. Add onions, celery, nuts, apples and mushrooms. Sauté and stir until mixture is lightly browned. Add salt and pepper to taste. Stuff crop and body cavities of roasting fowl and secure with string or trussing pins. (Enough for 2 chickens or a 6-pound turkey.)

# TAHITIAN CHICKEN LEGS

6 whole chicken legs, each cut into 2 parts
3 cups chicken broth
½ onion, cut into chunks
½ clove garlic, peeled
½ celery stalk
½ teaspoon salt

Combine chicken pieces, broth, onion, garlic, and celery. Simmer covered until almost tender. Add salt and continue simmering until tender. Remove chicken pieces to shallow serving dish and keep warm. Serve with sauce.

SAUCE:
½ cup white wine
1 cup chicken broth
1 tablespoon grated fresh ginger root
½ teaspoon turmeric powder
1 cup coconut milk (page 5)
Parsley

Put wine, broth, ginger root, and turmeric into saucepan and bring to simmering point. Simmer 5 minutes. Add coconut milk gradually, stirring constantly until hot but not boiling. Pour sauce over chicken and garnish with parsley. Serve with rice.

# HAWAIIAN CHICKEN LEGS

6 whole chicken legs, each cut into 2 parts

MARINADE:
¼ cup soy sauce
¼ cup honey
2 tablespoons rice vinegar
1 tablespoon brown sugar
¼ cup flour
¼ teaspoon paprika
¼ cup peanut oil

Place chicken pieces in a shallow bowl. Mix marinade ingredients thoroughly and pour over chicken. Roll pieces around in marinade and press mixture into pieces to saturate them. Cover and let stand at room temperature for 4 hours or in refrigerator overnight. Remove chicken pieces and drain. Put flour and paprika into a paper bag and shake chicken pieces, a few at a time, in the bag until coated with flour. Put oil into a baking pan. Put chicken pieces into pan, rolling them around to coat evenly with oil. Bake uncovered at 350° until tender. (Takes about half an hour.) (You may deep fry the pieces in 3 cups heated peanut oil for 10 minutes if you prefer.)

# PHILIPPINE CHICKEN WITH EGG

4 whole chicken legs
4 tablespoons peanut oil
1 onion, peeled, sliced
¼ cup flour
½ teaspoon paprika
⅛ teaspoon thyme
¼ teaspoon salt
¼ teaspoon pepper
2 hard-cooked eggs, peeled, chopped
¼ cup minced Chinese parsley (fresh coriander)

Put oil into heavy baking dish and heat until hot. Sauté onion slices until golden. Remove from fire and reserve onions. Put flour, paprika, thyme, salt, and pepper into a paper bag. Shake chicken pieces in bag, a few at a time, to coat with flour mixture. Lay chicken pieces in the baking dish, rolling them around to coat evenly with oil (add more if needed). Bake in 350° oven for 30 to 40 minutes until tender. Put onions back into dish for the last 5 minutes of baking time. Combine eggs and parsley and sprinkle over the chicken just before serving.

# FRICASSEE DE LAPIN

(NEW CALEDONIA)

1 (4 to 5 lb.) rabbit, cleaned and cut into serving pieces
    (reserve liver, chop, and add last 15 minutes)
½ cup flour to which 1 teaspoon each of salt and pepper have been
    added, for dredging
6 strips bacon, cut into 1-inch pieces
2 tablespoons butter
2 cups chicken stock
2 cups dry white wine
1 onion, chopped
1 clove garlic, crushed
½ teaspoon marjoram
1 tablespoon chopped parsley
2 tablespoons tomato paste
1 cup chopped mushrooms, fresh or canned
2 carrots, peeled and chopped
1 cup light cream
3 tablespoons cornstarch

Put dredging flour in small paper bag. Put two rabbit pieces at a time into bag and shake until well-coated with flour. Fry out bacon in heavy stew pot. Add butter. Fry rabbit pieces until well-browned. Add stock, white wine, onion, garlic, marjoram, parsley, tomato paste, mushrooms and carrots. Simmer covered 1½ hours until tender, adding chopped liver last 15 minutes. Transfer rabbit pieces to serving platter. Put cornstarch into cream and mix, then add to boiling sauce and stir until thickened. Serve sauce in separate bowl.

# POLYNESIAN RACK OF LAMB

   1 rack of lamb (allow 2 ribs per serving)
     Slivers of garlic
     Slices of peeled avocado
     Slices of green and red bell pepper
     Salt, pepper and flour

Cut pockets in rack between ribs about half-way through rack. In each pocket put 2 slivers of garlic, one slice each of green and red pepper and 2 slices of avocado. Tie rack up firmly with string. Dust with salt, pepper and flour. Roast 375° oven for 40 minutes.

# PAPEETE POT ROAST

   4 pounds beef pot roast (allow ½-lb. per serving)
  ½ cup flour
   1 teaspoon salt
  ½ teaspoon pepper
   4 tablespoons oil
   1 onion, stuck with 2 cloves
   2 stalks celery, cut in chunks
   1 leek, sliced (use white part only)
   2 cups hot water

Rub salt, pepper and flour into roast. Brown in hot oil in heavy stew pot. Add onion, celery and leek. Add hot water. Roast covered in 325° oven for 2½ to 3 hours or until tender. Slice and serve with Papeete Pois (page 76) and mashed potatoes.

# BEEF TERIYAKI

4 (3-oz.) top sirloin steaks (allow 1 per person), sliced ⅜-inch thick, trimmed of fat
¼ cup soy sauce
1 onion, sliced thick
2 celery stalks, cut into strips
1 green bell pepper, cut into strips
3 tablespoons peanut oil
¼ cup pineapple juice
1 cup pineapple chunks or 1 (8-oz.) can

Brush steaks with some of the soy sauce and set aside. Sauté onion, celery, and pepper in oil for 5 minutes. Add rest of soy sauce, pineapple juice, and pineapple chunks. Bring to a boil. Simmer 5 minutes. Cover and set aside, keeping warm. Broil steak to taste and remove to serving platter. Arrange steaks in the center of the platter and surround with vegetables.

# KOREAN BEEF RIBS

4 pounds beef short ribs, cut into 1½-inch lengths
2 cups water
8 small white boiling onions
8 stalks bok choy or Swiss chard, cut into 3-inch lengths

MARINADE:
½ cup soy sauce
2 tablespoons sugar
½ teaspoon pepper
¼ cup minced scallions
½ clove garlic, minced
¼ cup peanut oil

Make several horizontal cuts in each rib, cutting almost to bone. Marinate ribs for ½ hour. Remove. Brown in heavy stew pot. Add water. Add onions. Simmer covered for ½ hour. Add bok choy or chard. Cover and simmer until bok choy is tender.

# PINEAPPLE BEEF TERIYAKI

1½ pounds boneless sirloin steak, cut into bite-size pieces

MARINADE:
 ½ cup sugar
 ½ cup soy sauce
 1 garlic clove, peeled, crushed
 1 (1-inch) cube fresh ginger root, peeled, crushed
 1 tablespoon peanut oil
 1 tablespoon lemon juice
 ½ fresh pineapple, peeled, cut into 1-inch cubes

Put meat into a deep bowl. Combine marinade ingredients, mix well, and pour over meat. Stir until meat is well-coated. Cover. Refrigerate for an hour, stirring several times. Remove meat from marinade and drain. Thread beef and pineapple cubes alternately on skewers. Broil until done to taste, basting with marinade and turning the skewers as you broil.

# SPICY BEEF TONGUE

1 fresh beef tongue (3 pounds or more)

SAUCE:
   2 tablespoons peanut oil
   1 clove garlic, peeled, minced
   ¼ cup soy sauce
   2 tablespoons sugar
   ¼ teaspoon Chinese Five Spices (available in Oriental markets
         or see below)

Boil beef tongue in water to cover until tender. Cool. Peel and set aside. Sauté garlic in peanut oil until lightly browned. Add soy sauce, sugar, and spices. Simmer 3 minutes. Slice tongue in thin slices and place in shallow baking pan. Pour sauce over slices and bake uncovered for 15 minutes at 325°. Serve in sauce.

CHINESE FIVE SPICES:
To make 1½ tablespoons Chinese Five Spices:

50 peppercorns
   4 whole star anise
   2 teaspoons fennel seed
   4 (1-inch) pieces of cinnamon stick
12 whole cloves

Combine all ingredients and blend in blender until powdered.

# HAWAIIAN MEAT LOAF

1 pound ground beef
1 pound ground pork
1 pound ground veal
1 medium-size onion, chopped fine
4 slices of bread, soaked in milk and drained
3 eggs, beaten
2 teaspoons salt
½ teaspoon white pepper
1 cup macadamia nuts, chopped medium fine
1 cup seasoned tomato sauce or chili sauce
2 tablespoons chopped parsley
1 cup bouillon or meat stock

Put meat into large bowl with onion, bread, eggs, salt, pepper, nuts, and half of the tomato sauce. Mix and mix and mix with hands. Form into a loaf and place in a greased pan allowing space all around. Cover with the rest of the tomato sauce, sprinkle parsley on top, and pour bouillon around sides. Bake in 350° oven 1 hour or more until done. Baste every 15 minutes.

# LUAU PORK ROAST

4 pounds pork loin
2 medium-size onions, sliced
2 stalks celery, sliced
¼ cup peanut oil
1 cup pineapple juice or crushed pineapple and juice
3 tablespoons soy sauce
1 teaspoon dry mustard
1 teaspoon grated fresh ginger root
     or ½ teaspoon ground ginger

Put sliced onions and celery in bottom of greased roasting pan. Put roast on top, fat side up. Mix rest of ingredients thoroughly to make a sauce. Pour half of sauce over roast. Roast in 350° oven uncovered for 1½ hours, basting frequently with rest of sauce until it is all used. (Sauce can also be used for basting pork roasted on a grill.)

# ROAST PORK LOIN

3 pounds pork loin roast

MARINADE:
1½ teaspoons Chinese Five Spices (available in Oriental markets)
    or see (page 42)
6 tablespoons soy sauce
6 tablespoons hot water
3 tablespoons honey
½ teaspoon fresh ground pepper
6 cloves garlic, peeled, crushed

Cut between the bones of the roast to separate them, but do not cut all the way through. Put into a deep dish. Pour marinade over meat and turn and baste meat until marinade is well distributed. Set aside for 2 hours or more, then drain thoroughly. Put into a roasting pan uncovered, fat side up, and roast at 325° for 1½ hours or until tender.

# BARBECUED PORK

3 pounds boneless pork loin, cut into 1½-inch cubes
2 teaspoons salt
½ teaspoon pepper
½ teaspoon sage
3 tart apples, cut into slices ½-inch thick
4 tomatoes, cut in halves
3 dry onions, cut into slices ½-inch thick

BARBECUE SAUCE:
½ cup olive oil
½ cup vinegar
2 teaspoons sugar
1 teaspoon paprika
1 teaspoon dry mustard

Combine all ingredients in saucepan and simmer until sugar is dissolved. Mix salt, pepper and sage and dredge pork cubes with mixture. Arrange pork, apples, tomatoes and onions on skewers. Barbecue on grill, basting with sauce and turning often until meat is tender.

# PORK ADOBO

## (PORK CHUNKS IN VINEGAR & SOY SAUCE)

1½ pounds boneless pork shoulder, cubed
3 tablespoons vinegar
2 tablespoons soy sauce
¼ teaspoon pepper
1 clove garlic, peeled, minced
3 tablespoons lard
1½ cups water

Put pork cubes into a bowl. Add vinegar, soy sauce, pepper and garlic. Let stand for an hour, stirring occasionally. Put lard into heavy stew pot and heat until hot. Lift pork cubes out of bowl and brown in lard. Add marinade and cook for a few minutes. Add water, cover and simmer until pork is tender. Transfer pork to a warm platter. Turn heat up and reduce sauce to about half the original amount. Pour sauce over cubes and serve.

# CHAMORRO SPARERIBS

4 to 5 pounds spareribs

MARINADE:
½ cup soy sauce
2 tablespoons lemon juice
2 tablespoons sugar
¼ cup minced green onions
½ teaspoon minced hot green chili pepper

Combine ingredients and soak ribs, turning often to coat, for 2 hours. Broil over charcoal fire until brown.

# PINEAPPLE PORK CHOPS

6 loin pork chops, cut thick (allow 1 per serving)
2 tablespoons oil
1 large dry onion, sliced
6 slices fresh or canned pineapple
1 large green bell pepper, seeded and chopped
2 stalks celery, chopped
1 cup chicken broth

MARINADE:
1 cup soy sauce
1 clove garlic, peeled and minced
1 teaspoon grated fresh ginger root
     or ½ teaspoon ground ginger
½ teaspoon pepper
½ cup white wine

Trim fat from chops. Drench thoroughly in marinade and let soak for 1 hour. Drain, reserving marinade. Brown chops in oil in heavy roasting pan. Put 1 slice of onion on each chop. Top with pineapple slices. Add green pepper, celery and broth to marinade. Pour over chops. Bake covered in 350° oven 1 hour.

# SWEET-AND-SOUR PORK

½ pound cooked roast pork,
   cut into bite-size pieces
1 tablespoon soy sauce
1 tablespoon sherry
½ cup cornstarch
1½ cups peanut oil
 3 dried black mushrooms,
   soaked in hot water until soft,
   sliced into thin strips

1 green bell pepper, cut into
   1½-inch squares
1 small onion, quartered
1 can (8-oz.) pineapple chunks
2 cloves garlic, peeled, minced
1 (1-inch) piece fresh ginger root,
   peeled, sliced thin

SAUCE:
 1 cup water
1/3 cup sugar
1/3 cup vinegar
 1 tablespoon soy sauce

1 tablespoon cornstarch (mixed
   with 2 tablespoons cold water)
2 cups shredded Chinese
   celery-cabbage

Put pork pieces in bowl with sherry and soy sauce and marinate for ½ hour. Put the cornstarch in a bowl and dredge the soaked pork. Heat oil to deep frying temperature in wok or skillet. Drop pork pieces into oil and fry until golden. Drain on paper towels and set aside. Pour off all but a few tablespoons of the hot oil. Turn heat down a bit. Add mushroom strips, green pepper, onion, pineapple, garlic and ginger. Stir and fry for about 5 minutes. Set aside. Make the sauce by combining all ingredients except cornstarch in a sauce-pan. Bring to a boil and stir for a few minutes, then add the cornstarch to thicken the mixture. Set aside. Put vegetable mixture back on high even heat. Add pork. Add sauce. Stir and fry for just long enough to mix all ingredients well. Serve hot with a bowl of shredded Chinese celery-cabbage.

# COURT BOUILLON FOR POACHING FISH

For poaching whole fish, fillets or steaks, you will need a poaching liquid or court bouillon. The amount of bouillon needed may vary but the procedure is the same. This recipe makes enough for 3 pounds of fish.

    1 pint dry white wine
    2 quarts water
    3 or 4 sprigs parsley
    1 onion, stuck with 2 cloves
    2 teaspoons salt
    1 bay leaf
    1 stalk celery, with leaves, chopped
   10 peppercorns
   ½ fresh lemon, sliced
   ¼ teaspoon thyme

Put all ingredients into large kettle and bring to a boil. Turn down heat and simmer for 30 minutes. Strain. To poach fish: Put enough bouillon to cover fish into a shallow pan or skillet. Bring to a boil. Add fish, turn down heat and simmer gently until fish flakes easily when tested with a fork. This will take 5 to 6 minutes per pound or a little longer if fish is thick. Remove and serve hot or cold, or with a sauce.

# BEC DE CAEN ROLLS
(NEW CALEDONIA POACHED SNAPPER)

2 pounds red snapper fillets
1 quart court bouillon (page 52)
2 cups bechamel sauce
½ cup minced parsley
½ lemon, sliced thin

BECHAMEL SAUCE
4 tablespoons butter
4 tablespoons flour
2 cups milk
1 teaspoon salt
½ teaspoon pepper

Melt butter in heavy saucepan. Remove from fire and blend in flour. Return to fire. Add milk slowly, stirring constantly until sauce is thick and smooth. Add salt and pepper.

Cut fillets lengthwise into 1½-inch-wide strips. Form each strip into a roll and secure with a toothpick. Poach carefully in court bouillon for 10 minutes. Remove with slotted spoon. Place in shallow baking dish. Cover with sauce. Sprinkle with parsley. Bake 15 minutes at 325°. Add lemon slices just before serving.

# OPAKAPAKA WITH SESAME
(HAWAIIAN POACHED SNAPPER)

2 pounds snapper fillets
1 (1-inch) piece of fresh ginger root
1 teaspoon salt
2 tablespoons sesame seeds
4 teaspoons peanut oil
¼ cup soy sauce
Pinch of pepper
½ cup chopped scallions

Put enough water to cover fillets into saucepan. Add ginger root and salt. Bring to a boil. Add fillets. Turn heat down, cover, and poach until fish is tender. Lift fish out and place on warm serving platter to keep warm. Spread sesame seeds in pie tin and toast in 300° oven for 10 minutes. Put them into a mortar and grind them to powder. Put peanut oil into small frying pan together with sesame powder, soy sauce, and pepper. Stir and heat until hot. Pour over fish. Sprinkle with scallions.

# MAHIMAHI WITH SHELLFISH SAUCE

2 pounds mahi mahi fillets
1 teaspoon salt

SAUCE:
  2 tablespoons butter or margarine
  2 tablespoons flour
  1 cup fish stock
  1 cup half-and-half
  ¼ cup grated Gruyère
     Pinch cayenne pepper
  ½ cup flaked cooked crab meat
  ½ cup chopped cooked shrimp
  1 tablespoon sherry

Poach fish in court bouillon (page 52). Remove and place on warm platter in warm place. Reserve liquid. Melt butter in saucepan. Add flour, stirring constantly until mixed and bubbly. Add 1 cup of the reserved fish stock and stir and cook for a few minutes. Add milk and cook and stir until sauce is thickened. Add cheese, cayenne, crab meat, shrimp, and sherry and stir well. Pour sauce over fish. Bake at 350° for 20 minutes.

# BROILED FISH

2 pounds fillets of any firm white fish
  Salt and pepper to taste
  Peanut oil
3 tablespoons fine bread crumbs
3 tablespoons ground macadamia nuts
¼ cup melted butter
3 tablespoons lemon juice
  Parsley

Sprinkle fillets with salt and pepper. Dredge in peanut oil, then in crumbs. Pat crumbs into fish. Broil under medium heat for 5 to 10 minutes on each side or until fish flakes easily when tested with a fork. Remove to serving platter. Sprinkle with macadamia nuts. Combine melted butter and lemon juice and pour over fish. Top with sprigs of parsley.

# DEVILED FISH
(BROILED FISH WITH HOT SAUCE)

4 quarter-pound snapper or sea bass fillets
  (allow 1 per person)

SAUCE:

- 2 teaspoons chopped scallions
- ½ teaspoon soy sauce
- ½ teaspoon Worcestershire sauce
  Few drops sesame oil
- 1 teaspoon Chinese prepared mustard
- 1 tablespoon peanut oil

Mix sauce ingredients in order given. Brush the fillets with the sauce on both sides. Broil until fish flakes easily when tested with a fork.

# HAWAIIAN OPAKAPAKA
## (SNAPPER IN COCONUT CREAM)

- 2 pounds red snapper fillets
- 1 tablespoon coarse salt
- 1 cup coconut cream (page 5)
- 3 tablespoons white wine
- 1 lemon, sliced thin
- 1 grapefruit, peeled, cut in sections
- 1 orange, peeled, cut in sections

Rub both sides of each fillet with salt. Put into shallow baking dish in single layer. Pour coconut cream over fillets, spreading evenly. Add white wine. Bake 350° for 20 minutes, basting several times. Serve on platter surrounded by fruit sections and lemon slices.

# BOUILLABAISSE A LA NOUMEA
(NEW CALEDONIA SEAFOOD STEW)

(Allow 1 pound per serving of combined total pounds of fish and shellfish)
  4 pounds assorted fresh fish:
    *salt-water* red snapper, halibut, haddock, cod, sea bass,
      flounder or sole
    *fresh-water* perch, pike, trout or bass
  2 pounds assorted lobster, or hard-shelled crab (cooked, cleaned,
    split, cut into large serving pieces)
  1 dozen clams or mussels, or ½ dozen of each
  2 large dry onions, coarsely chopped
  1 large leek, sliced (use white part only)
  2 cloves garlic, mashed
  2 fresh tomatoes, chopped
  ½ cup olive oil
  1 strip orange peel
  ½ teaspoon basil
  1 tablespoon salt
  ½ teaspoon pepper
    Pinch of powdered saffron
  2 quarts boiling water
  2 cups white wine
  ½ cup minced parsley (for garnish)

CROUTONS:
  1 loaf French bread      1 clove garlic, mashed
  1 stick (4-oz.) butter      Salt

Cut bread into 1½-inch-thick slices. Mix mashed garlic with butter and spread evenly on bread. Cut slices into 1½-inch-thick squares to form cubes. Put on cookie sheet butter-side-up. Sprinkle with salt. Bake 350° until brown.

Scale, gut and wash fish. Discard gills and heads. Cut large fish crosswise into 2-inch-wide slices. Scrub clams and mussels in cold running water. Put lobster and crab in one container, fish in another, clams and mussels in another. Put onions, leek, garlic and tomatoes in large deep kettle. Add olive oil and all seasonings. Stir well. Add boiling water and white wine. Boil uncovered 10 minutes. Add fish, lobster and crab. Boil uncovered for 12 minutes. Add clams and mussels and boil until their shells open. Remove all fish and shellfish carefully with tongs or slotted spoon. Set aside on warm platter in warm place. Strain stock and pour into soup plates. Sprinkle with parsley. Serve croutons with soup. Remove soup plates. Serve individual portions of the various kinds of fish and shellfish.

# OPAKAPAKA WITH DILL SAUCE
(BAKED SNAPPER)

2 pounds snapper fillets
2 tablespoons butter
2 tablespoons flour
1½ cups half-and-half

1 tablespoon chopped fresh dill
   or 1 teaspoon dried dill weed
Salt and pepper to taste

Poach fish in court bouillon (page 52). Remove and place in shallow baking dish. Melt butter in saucepan. Add flour, stirring well until mixture is bubbly. Add milk gradually, stirring constantly until sauce comes to a boil and is thickened. Add dill and stir. Pour sauce over fish. Bake at 350° for 10 minutes.

# SEAFOOD SAUCES
## (SERVE WITH COOKED SHRIMP, PRAWNS, CRAYFISH OR LOBSTER)

SAUCE 1 (Papeete, Tahiti)
  2 tablespoons butter or margarine
  2 tablespoons flour
1½ cups coconut milk (page 5)
  ½ teaspoon salt
  ½ teaspoon pepper
  2 teaspoons curry powder
  ½ cup chopped mushrooms

Melt butter. Add flour and blend. Add coconut milk slowly, stirring constantly until sauce is thick and smooth. Add seasonings and mushrooms.

SAUCE 2 (Noumea, New Caledonia)
  2 tablespoons butter or margarine
  2 tablespoons flour
1½ cups coconut milk (page 5)
  ½ teaspoon salt
  ½ teaspoon pepper
  1 tablespoon tomato paste
  ½ cup sour cream
    Minced chives or scallions for topping

Melt butter. Add flour and blend. Add coconut milk slowly, stirring constantly until sauce is thick and smooth. Add seasonings and tomato paste. Pour over cooked seafood. Spread sour cream on top of sauce. Sprinkle with chives or scallions.

# JAPANESE TEMPURA
(WITH SHRIMP AND VEGETABLES)

Prepare the following ingredients and put on large trays lined with absorbent paper. Allow 2 each of the following per serving:

Prawns or jumbo shrimp (clean, devein, leave tails on)
Squid (clean, split lengthwise, cut in triangular-shaped pieces 2 inches wide at bottom) Allow 2 triangles per serving.
Zucchini, cut in ½-inch-thick slices
Green beans, cut in 4-inch-long pieces
Sweet potatoes, cut in ½-inch-thick slices
Cauliflower (cut fleurettes off, then cut them lengthwise in ½-inch-thick slices)
Large mushrooms, cut in ¼-inch-thick slices vertically
Asparagus tips
Carrots, peeled and cut diagonally in ½-inch-thick slices
Japanese eggplant, cut in 3-inch-long pieces, then cut in half
Green bell pepper, cut in 1×2-inch pieces
3 cups peanut or corn oil for deep-frying

BATTER:  1 egg, beaten      1 cup ice water      1 cup flour

Beat egg in bowl. Add ice water and beat. Sift flour in, mixing and stirring as you add. Do not stir after batter is mixed. Leave it rather lumpy.

Heat oil to deep-fry temperature (375°) in large deep frying pan. Flour prawns or shrimp lightly before dipping. Dip each ingredient in batter, coating it completely and drop into oil. Deep fry, 6 or 8 pieces at a time, until pale gold and crisp. Remove with slotted spoon or tongs and immediately place on absorbent paper to drain. Put finished pieces on cookie sheets lined with absorbent paper in warm oven until you complete frying. Tempura pieces can be fried ahead of time, then re-heated on rack in 300° oven for 5 or 10 minutes just before serving.

# TEMPURA DIPPING SAUCES
(SERVE ½ CUP SAUCE IN SMALL BOWL WITH EACH SERVING OF TEMPURA)

SAUCE 1:
   3 cups dashi (Japanese soup stock). Packaged dashi mix is available in most large grocery or Oriental food stores. If unavailable, make your own as follows: Bring 3 cups water to a boil. Add 1 cup katsuobushi (dried fish shavings), a 3-inch-square piece of kombu (seaweed) and ¼ teaspoon seasoned salt. Turn heat off. Let stand 10 minutes. Strain.
   ½ cup soy sauce
   ½ cup mirin (sweet sake)
   1 teaspoon seasoned salt
   1 cup grated daikon (Japanese radish) or white icicle radish

Mix all ingredients except radish in order given. Bring to a boil. Turn off heat. Just before serving put 1 teaspoonful grated radish in each dipping bowl.

SAUCE 2:
   3 cups water                         1½ teaspoons sugar
   1 cup soy sauce                      Pinch of powdered ginger
   3 tablespoons sake or sherry

Mix all ingredients in sauce pan. Bring to a boil. Turn off heat.

# STEAMBOATS AND HOT POTS

There are many versions of a steaming one-pot dish that is popular through-out the Pacific islands, known as the Fiji Steamboat, the Chinese Hot Pot, and the (Japanese) Shabu-shabu. Each of these is something like a soup and a stew, a steaming broth into which small amounts of meat, fowl, seafood, vegetables, and noodles are cooked, a few at a time. (Cooking times vary from 2 to 5 minutes.) The ingredients are readied in advance and set out in small bowls around the cooking pot. Each diner cooks his food when he likes and as long as he likes and then fishes it out with a wire scoop or long-handled strainer. The pieces of food are usually eaten with chopsticks, and as a last course, noodles of some kind are cooked in the broth, then served with it in bowls.

The Fiji Steamboat gets its name from the pot in which it is cooked, a large round metal vessel with an inverse funnel-shaped center. The pot is filled with cooking liquid and set to simmer over a charcoal fire during the meal. (The Steamboat is a Chinese-type hot pot.) The Shabu-shabu pot is an or-dinary stew pot, sometimes electrified. There is satisfaction in using the authentic hot pots, but if you are indoors it is easier and safer to cook these delicacies in a cast-iron pot on a hot plate.

Put the hot plate in the center of the table or on a coffee table or — best of all — on the floor, keep the broth simmering, and dip away. Every shrimp, every piece of chicken, every scallion or mushroom that anyone cooks contributes to the final flavor of the soup, a communal triumph.

(Each of the following recipes will serve 6.)

64

# FIJI STEAMBOAT

  2 quarts chicken broth
½ cup sherry
¼ cup soy sauce
  3 teaspoons grated ginger root
  2 tablespoons Dijon-style mustard
  6 ounces cellophane noodles (bean threads)
¼ pound boneless fresh, firm white fish, cubed
  1 dozen medium-sized prawns, shelled, deveined
½ dozen scallops, cut into bite-size pieces
  1 cooked crab, cleaned, broken into serving pieces, cracked
  1 chicken breast, boned and cut into bite-size pieces
½ of a celery cabbage, washed, leaves separated
  1 (6-oz.) cake of fresh tofu (soy bean curd) cut into bite-size cubes
    Bunch of watercress, washed

Put the noodles into a pan, cover with boiling water, let stand 30 minutes to soften, drain and set aside. Put chicken broth, sherry, soy sauce, ginger root, and mustard into cooking pot. Bring to a simmer on a hot plate. Distribute the ingredients in small bowls and let diners cook what they please. At the end of the meal, add noodles to broth and simmer 5 minutes. Serve bowls of broth with noodles.

# CHINESE HOT POT

1½ pounds lamb leg or top sirloin beef
½ pound celery-cabbage
½ pound fresh spinach, washed
6 ounces cellophane noodles (bean threads)
1 cake fresh tofu (6-oz.), cut into bite-size cubes
2 quarts chicken broth

DIPPING SAUCE:
3 tablespoons chopped scallions
3 teaspoons minced Chinese parsley (fresh coriander)
3 tablespoons sesame seeds, toasted for 10 minutes in 300° oven,
    then ground fine
3 tablespoons sesame oil
½ cup soy sauce
½ cup peanut oil
½ cup wine vinegar
3 teaspoons sugar

Cut meat against the grain into ⅛-inch-thick slices. Wash celery cabbage and spinach. Put noodles into deep bowl, cover with boiling water, let stand 30 minutes to soften, then drain and set aside. Put all the food into bowls and arrange around the hot pot. Put broth into pot and bring to simmering. Combine all dipping sauce ingredients in a bowl and blend. Pour into individual dipping bowls. Cook a few meat slices first, dip and eat them, then alternate with the vegetables and bean curd. When meat and vegetables are gone, add the noodles to the broth and serve in soup bowls.

# SHABU-SHABU
(JAPANESE HOT POT)

6 cups beef broth
½ cup soy sauce
4 tablespoons sherry
3 eggs
6 ounces Oriental egg noodles
12 fresh mushrooms, washed or wiped carefully with paper towel
6 green onions, roots trimmed, cut in half
½ pound fresh spinach, washed
1½ pounds boneless lean beef, cut across the grain in ⅛-inch-thick slices
1 cake tofu (bean curd) (6-oz.), cut into bite-size cubes

DIPPING SAUCE:

| | |
|---|---|
| 1/3 cup sesame seeds | 1 teaspoon sugar |
| 1/3 cup cooking broth | 1 tablespoon sherry |
| 3 tablespoons rice vinegar | 1 tablespoon soy sauce |

Prepare the mushrooms, onions, spinach, beef, and tofu and put in bowls around the cooking pot. Put the beef broth, soy sauce, and sherry into the pot and simmer. Drop the eggs into boiling water in a saucepan. Boil 5 minutes, run cold water over them to cool, and set aside in hot water. For the dipping sauce, toast the sesame seeds in a pie tin in a 300° oven for 10 minutes. Grind them fine in a mortar and combine with the rice vinegar, sugar, sherry, soy sauce, and 1/3 cup of the cooking broth. Blend thoroughly and pour into small bowls for dipping. Cook the noodles three minutes in boiling water, stirring occasionally, then serve in six soup plates. Peel the warm eggs and put half an egg into each plate. The diners then cook individual portions of meat and vegetables to eat with the noodles and eggs. When everything is gone, serve the broth.

# OUTDOOR SMOKER—GRILL RECIPES

Mainlanders are not apt to have underground ovens as many islanders do, but an ideal way to simulate that long, slow steaming-roasting method of cooking is to use one of the smoker-cookers now available. These heavy duty cookers can be used as charcoal grills, or with the domed lid in place, as steamers or ovens and will handle up to 20 pounds of meat, fowl or seafood. They are equipped with a water pan which fits between the charcoal pan and the grill. The water moderates the heat and keeps the food moist as it cooks. For smoked flavor, you add a handful of water-soaked hickory or fruitwood chips to the coals before cooking. The cooking procedure is the same for all the following recipes — only the number of hours is different. Put charcoal in the fire pan, add soaked chips, put water pan in place and fill with water. Put grill in place with food on it, cover and cook for the number of hours specified in the recipe.

# ROAST BEEF

4 pounds beef rump roast

MARINADE:
¾ cup soy sauce
¾ cup sherry
1 cup water

3 cloves garlic, minced
1 (1-inch) piece fresh ginger, peeled, minced

Soak roast in marinade covered in a cool place for 3 or 4 hours (or overnight) turning several times. Roast as above for about 5 hours.

# ROAST PORK

4 pounds pork loin

MARINADE:
¾ cup soy sauce
¾ cup bourbon
1 cup honey
3 tablespoons sugar
1 teaspoon pepper
1 teaspoon salt
Few drops sesame oil

Soak roast in marinade covered in a cool place for 3 or 4 hours (or overnight) turning several times. Roast for about 5 hours (page 70).

# ROAST CHICKEN

4-5 pound roasting capon

MARINADE:
½ cup soy sauce
1½ cups white wine
½ cup lemon juice
1 clove garlic, peeled, crushed

72

Put chicken into a plastic bag with the marinade and let it soak for a few hours. Take chicken out and reserve marinade for water pan.

Stuff chicken with:
  1 medium-size onion, quartered
  3 stalks celery with leaves, cut into chunks

Put marinade into water pan and roast for about 5 hours (page 70).

# ROAST FISH

3-4 pounds fish steaks cut thick (swordfish, salmon or halibut)

MARINADE:
  ½ cup soy sauce
  ½ cup white wine
  ½ cup lemon juice

Lay fish steaks in marinade in shallow dish. Cover and refrigerate for 3 to 4 hours. Follow roasting procedure (page 70) but roast only 2 to 3 hours or until fish flakes easily with fork when tested.

# LAU LAUS
(PACKETS OF MEAT AND FISH IN LEAVES)

HAWAIIAN:
   1 pound fresh butterfish, mackerel or salmon fillets. (Sprinkle with
      1½ tablespoons salt and let stand for ½ hour before using.)
   2 pounds fresh spinach
   2 pounds pork butt
      Pepper and lemon juice
   8 (12-inch-square) pieces of aluminum foil

Prepare fish. When ready, rinse and drain thoroughly. Divide into 8 portions.
Wash, drain and remove stems from spinach leaves. Make 8 piles of 1 dozen
leaves each. Cut pork into 8 slices. Cut foil squares and lay on flat surface,
shiny side down. Lay 6 spinach leaves, largest ones on bottom, on each
square. Put 1 slice of pork on each pile, then 1 portion of fish, then 6 more
spinach leaves, smallest ones first. Sprinkle with pepper and a few drops of
lemon juice. Bring corners of each foil packet together on top to form a round
bag, then twist foil ends together tightly at center top. Set on rack in steamer
with about 2 inches of water in bottom. Steam 3 hours. Remove foil, pour off
excess juice and serve hot.


TONGAN:
   2 pounds fresh spinach
   8 (inch-thick) slices canned corned beef
   8 tablespoons coconut milk (page 5)

Prepare packets as above using these three ingredients. Put meat slices on
leaves, then 1 tablespoon coconut milk, then rest of leaves. Steam 1½ hours.

75

# PAPEETE POIS

1 package (8-oz.) split peas, soaked overnight in 6 cups water, drained
4 cups water
1 medium-size onion, chopped
2 stalks celery, chopped
2 smoked ham hocks
Salt and pepper to taste

Put drained split peas in deep soup pot with 4 cups water, onion, celery and ham hocks. Bring to a boil, turn heat to low, cover and simmer for 2 to 3 hours until quite thick. Stir frequently once it starts to thicken. Remove ham hocks, discard skin and bones, chop meat and put back in pot. Put through a colander or food mill. Add salt and pepper. Cool. Serve individual portions in vegetable dishes.

# PHILIPPINE GREEN BEANS

½ pound finely chopped pork
1 clove garlic, peeled, minced
1 tablespoon soy sauce
1 cup water
1 pound Chinese long beans (or green string beans) cut in
    1½-inch pieces
1 small tomato, seeded, chopped
    Peanut oil for frying

Fry pork in large frying pan until brown. Add garlic and fry 2 minutes more. Add soy sauce and water. Bring to a boil. Add beans. Cook until beans are just barely tender. Add tomato. Stir. Serve hot.

# PAN FRIED CABBAGE
(PHILIPPINE STYLE)

½ cup finely cut boneless pork loin
5 cups finely shredded cabbage
1 teaspoon salt
  Peanut oil for frying

Heat oil until hot in large frying pan. Add pork and fry until brown. Add cabbage and salt. Stir and fry for 4 to 5 minutes. Do not overcook.


# GUAMANIAN POTATO SALAD

6 potatoes
6 hard-cooked eggs
6 scallions, chopped
½ cup pitted, sliced green olives
1 (2-oz.) can pimentos, drained, chopped
1 teaspoon salt
½ teaspoon pepper
½ cup mayonnaise

Boil potatoes with skins on until tender. Cool, peel and slice into salad bowl. Peel and slice eggs. Add onions, olives, pimentos, salt and pepper and mix. Add mayonnaise and mix.

# HOT PAPAYA CHUTNEY

1 fresh papaya, peeled, seeded, coarsely chopped
1½ cups chopped fresh pineapple
½ cup raisins
1 (2-inch) cube of fresh ginger root, peeled, minced
2/3 cup vinegar
2 cups brown sugar
2 cloves garlic, peeled, minced fine
½ teaspoon crushed red chili pepper
1 teaspoon salt
½ teaspoon cloves
½ cup blanched, slivered almonds

Boil sugar and vinegar for 10 minutes. Add rest of ingredients and bring to a boil. Turn heat down and simmer until thick, stirring constantly. Can be put into sterilized jelly jars while hot and sealed for storage. Makes 2 glasses.

# TOMATO CHUTNEY

6 large ripe tomatoes, peeled, chopped
1 large dry onion, peeled, chopped
¼ cup raisins, chopped
2 green apples, peeled, chopped
1 cup sugar
1 tablespoon minced hot green chilies, fresh or canned
2 cups vinegar

Put all ingredients in heavy saucepan. Stir constantly over low heat until sugar is dissolved. Simmer, stirring often, until fruit is soft and mixture is thick. Takes an hour or more. Makes 3 cups.

# CABBAGE TSUKEMONO
(JAPANESE PICKLED CABBAGE)

1 small head green cabbage
½ teaspoon salt
1 cup sugar
½ cup vinegar

Slice cabbage into ½-inch-wide strips and put into shallow dish. Combine salt, sugar, and vinegar and boil for 1 minute, stirring until sugar is dissolved. Cool. Pour over cabbage strips. Let stand overnight in refrigerator.

# LEMON-ONION CHUTNEY

3 lemons
4 tablespoons minced light raisins
1 medium-size dry onion, peeled, chopped
2 tablespoons minced green chilies, fresh or canned
2 cups sugar
1 tablespoon salt
1½ cups vinegar

Squeeze lemons. Strain juice into deep bowl. Discard seeds and pulp. Slice lemon rinds into thin slices and put in bowl. Add raisins, onions and chilies. Let stand 3 hours. Put in saucepan with sugar, salt and vinegar. Stir over low heat until sugar is dissolved. Simmer until thick. Takes about 1½ hours. Makes 3 cups.

# HEARTS OF PALM
(WITH SAUCE VINAIGRETTE)

1 pound fresh hearts of palm
    or 1 (14-oz.) can hearts of palm
½ cup fresh lemon juice
1 cup sauce vinaigrette

SAUCE VINAIGRETTE:
3 tablespoons red wine vinegar
6 tablespoons olive oil
3 tablespoons minced parsley, chives or scallions
¼ teaspoon dry mustard
¼ teaspoon salt
⅛ teaspoon pepper

Beat oil into vinegar slowly. Add rest of ingredients. Mix well.

Peel and cut hearts into ½-inch-wide strips. Cover with lemon juice. Let stand 5 minutes. Boil in small amount of water until tender. (Canned hearts need no cooking, just drain and cut into strips.) Add sauce vinaigrette. Chill. (Serves 6.)

# BEAN SPROUT SALAD

1 pound fresh bean sprouts
1 bunch watercress
3 tablespoons sugar
3 tablespoons white vinegar
2 tablespoons salad oil
1 tablespoon lemon juice
½ teaspoon salt
¼ teaspoon pepper

Wash sprouts and drain. Cover with water. Bring to a boil and stir and cook 1 minute. Drain and cool. Wash cress and break into pieces. Put into shallow bowl. Add sprouts to cress. Mix sugar, vinegar, oil, lemon juice, salt, and pepper. Pour dressing over cress and sprout mixture. Refrigerate overnight. Stir and serve crisp and cold.

# STUFFED PAPAYA

2 fresh papayas (allow ½ papaya per person)
½ pound cooked, minced ham
¼ teaspoon ground cloves
2 tablespoons brandy
Fresh lettuce or spinach leaves

Cut papayas into halves. Scoop out seeds with spoon. Combine ham, cloves and brandy. Mix thoroughly. Stuff papaya halves with ham mixture packing it in firmly. Cover and chill for a couple of hours. Serve on a bed of lettuce or spinach leaves. Serve with papaya seed dressing.

# PAPAYA SEED DRESSING

½ cup sugar
½ cup wine vinegar
1 tablespoon fresh lemon juice
½ teaspoon salt
½ teaspoon dry mustard
1 cup salad oil
3 tablespoons minced red onion
1 heaping tablespoon papaya seeds

Put all ingredients into a blender in order given. Blend 20 seconds or until papaya seeds are the size of coarse pepper. Good with fruit or tossed green salads. Makes 1½ cups.

# HAWAIIAN IMPERIAL SALAD

2 chicken breasts, boned
3 tablespoons soy sauce
3 tablespoons whiskey (bourbon)
  or sherry
A (1½-inch-square) cube of
  fresh ginger root, peeled
  and crushed or ¾ teaspoon
  ground ginger
½ cup water chestnut flour,
  or cornstarch
½ teaspoon salt
1 cup peanut oil for deep-frying
1 head iceberg lettuce,
  shredded fine (about 6 cups)

1 teaspoon sesame oil
4 scallions, chopped
1 tablespoon prepared mustard
1 cup Chinese rice sticks
  (Py Mei Fun) broken into
  2-inch lengths, deep-fried
½ cup macadamia nuts, browned
  in 1 tablespoon oil, chopped
½ cup minced Chinese parsley
  (cilantro), or watercress
Salt and pepper to taste

Make a marinade of soy sauce, whiskey and ginger. Soak chicken in it for ½ hour. Remove chicken and coat heavily with flour, patting additional flour into chicken pieces with hands. Lay pieces on rack over steam in covered steamer for 5 minutes to set flour. Remove. Add salt. Heat oil to 375° in heavy frying pan. Deep-fry rice sticks, small handfuls at a time. Remove each handful after about 1 minute, with slotted spoon and set aside to cool and drain on absorbent paper. Fry chicken until good and brown (4 to 5 minutes to a side). Remove and set aside to cool. Put shredded lettuce in deep salad bowl. Add sesame oil, scallions and mustard and mix well. Shred chicken and add. Add rice sticks. Put 1 tablespoon oil in small frying pan with the macadamia nuts and heat until oil is hot. Brown the nuts, turning once. Remove, cool and chop. Add to salad. Add parsley. Toss. Add salt and pepper to taste. (Serves 8.)

# ORIENTAL RICE

2 cups rice, rinsed three times in cold water
   (allow 1/3 cup raw rice per serving)
3 cups water

Put rinsed rice into deep, heavy-bottomed pan with tight lid. Add water. Bring to a boil uncovered and let boil until water is almost down to rice level. Turn heat down low. Cover tightly. Cook 15 to 20 minutes or until water is absorbed.

# ORIENTAL NOODLES

FRESH: Thin, round, 1/8-inch-wide noodles made of flour, egg and water. Can be frozen. Cook as you would regular egg noodles according to package directions. Dried Chinese egg noodles can be substituted. Prepare them according to package directions.

CELLOPHANE: Very thin brittle thread-like noodles made from ground mung beans. Packaged in skeins, labelled bean thread. Become translucent when cooked. Allow 1 ounce of uncooked noodles per serving. To prepare: Cover with boiling water and let stand for an hour. Drain. Cut into 4-inch lengths. Measure equal amounts of noodles and water. Put into saucepan. Bring to a boil. Turn heat down to lowest heat and simmer gently until tender.

CHINESE RICE NOODLES (long rice): Thin, thread-like noodles made of ground rice. Packaged in skeins, labelled rice sticks. Resemble cellophane noodles before and after cooking. Allow 1 ounce of uncooked noodles per serving. Prepare exactly as you would cellophane noodles.

# HAWAIIAN FRIED RICE

2 cups cooked, diced chicken, pork or shrimp
2 tablespoons peanut oil
1 (2½-oz.) can mushroom pieces
4 cups cold cooked rice
1 tablespoon minced onion
3 tablespoons soy sauce
½ teaspoon salt
2 eggs, beaten
2 tablespoons chopped pimentos
½ green bell pepper, minced
2 tablespoons minced scallions

Sauté chicken in oil until brown. Add mushrooms, rice, onion, soy sauce and salt. Stir well and cook 10 minutes. Add beaten eggs slowly, stirring and tossing rice until eggs are cooked. Put pimentos, green pepper and scallions in bottom of round, shallow bowl. Turn fried rice out over these ingredients and press rice down hard with spatula. Put a platter face-down on top of bowl. Holding platter tight to bowl, reverse it and remove bowl. (Serves 6.)

# SPANISH RICE

2 teaspoons ground achiote seeds
2 tablespoons peanut oil
1 onion, peeled, chopped
2 cloves garlic, peeled, minced
½ pound pork sausages, cut into ¼-inch slices
1 cup tomato sauce
2 cups chicken broth
1 teaspoon salt
½ teaspoon pepper
2 cups rice, rinsed well in cold water
1 cup fresh green peas

Achiote seeds are small, brick-red colored seeds from the annatto tree. They can be bought in Latin American markets. To prepare: Put ¼ cup of seeds into saucepan with ½ cup water. Boil for 5 minutes, set aside and let soak overnight. Drain, dry and grind fine in a mortar.

Heat oil until hot. Add ground achiote seeds and fry for 2 minutes. Remove from heat, strain oil into heavy stew pot. Sauté onion and garlic for a few minutes, add sausages and fry until brown. Add tomato sauce, broth, salt, pepper, peas and rice. Stir well. Cover and bake at 350° for 30 to 40 minutes or until rice has absorbed liquid.

# PANCIT

(NOODLES WITH PORK, SHRIMP & CHICKEN)

½ cup sliced Chinese black mushrooms
5 tablespoons peanut oil
1 small onion, peeled, chopped
1 clove garlic, peeled, minced
1 teaspoon salt
1 cup roasted pork strips (½-inch thick)
1 cup boiled chicken strips (½-inch thick)
1 cup chopped cooked shrimp
1 cup thin slices of celery
1 cup shredded celery-cabbage or cabbage
2 cups chicken stock
½ pound pancit (Chinese egg noodles)
    Lemon juice
2 sliced hard cooked eggs

Cover mushrooms with water and let soak 15 minutes or more. Drain and pat dry with paper towel. Heat 3 tablespoons of oil in heavy saucepan or skillet. Add onion, garlic and salt. Sauté until onion is yellow. Add pork, chicken, and shrimp. Slice mushrooms and add. Stir and fry for 3 minutes. Add celery and celery-cabbage. Stir and remove from heat. Cover and keep warm. Bring broth to a boil. Add noddles and cook until just tender. Drain thoroughly in sieve or colander. Heat remining 2 tablespoons of oil in frying pan. Add noodles and stir and fry until noodles are coated with oil and slightly brown. Put noodles in mound on platter. Pour first mixture over noodles. Sprinkle with lemon juice. Garnish with egg slices.

# SOTANGHON

(NOODLES WITH PORK AND VEGETABLES)

4 ounces sotanghon (Oriental cellophane noodles)
½ cup sliced Chinese black mushrooms
2 tablespoons peanut oil
1 clove garlic, peeled, minced
1 cup chopped roast pork
1 cup chopped cooked shrimp
1 cup chopped cooked chicken
2 carrots, scraped, cut into thin strips
1 cup shredded cabbage
1 cup water
2 tablespoons soy sauce
½ cup chopped scallions

Soak noodles in water to cover for 1 hour. Drain thoroughly when ready to use. Soak mushrooms in warm water to cover for 15 minutes. Drain and pat dry with paper towel, then slice. Heat oil in heavy saucepan or skillet. Sauté garlic and onion until brown. Add pork, shrimp, chicken and mushrooms. Stir and fry for 1 minute. Add water and soy sauce and bring to a boil. Add noodles slowly. Add cabbage and carrots. Turn down heat and simmer until noodles are just tender. Sprinkle each serving with chopped scallions.

# TWICE-FRIED NOODLES

½ pound boneless pork, cut into thin strips

MARINADE:
   1 clove garlic, peeled, crushed
   ½ inch piece of fresh ginger root, peeled, minced
   1 tablespoon sherry
   1 teaspoon sugar
   2 tablespoons soy sauce

NOODLES:
   ½ pound Chinese egg noodles
1½ quarts boiling water
   ½ teaspoon salt
   3 tablespoons peanut oil
   1 tablespoon soy sauce
   1 cup diagonally-sliced green beans
   6 water chestnuts, sliced
   ½ cup bamboo shoots
   6 scallions, cut into 2-inch lengths
   1 cup chicken bouillon
   1 tablespoon cornstarch
   1 tablespoon soy sauce

Put pork strips into a bowl. Mix garlic, ginger, sherry, sugar, and soy sauce and pour over pork. Let stand ½ hour. While the meat is marinating, prepare noodles by cooking, uncovered, for 3 or 4 minutes in boiling salted water for 5 minutes. Drain. Rinse with cold water. Heat 2 tablespoons of oil in a frying pan. Add noodles. Flatten them with a spatula and fry until slightly brown on the bottom. Turn as you would a pancake and press down again. Fry until brown on the bottom. Sprinkle with soy sauce. Repeat frying and browning a second time so that the noodles are quite crisp. Set aside and keep warm. Heat 1 tablespoon of oil in a heavy frying pan. Add pork and marinade. Cook, stirring and frying, for 5 minutes. Add carrots, green beans, water chestnuts, and bamboo shoots. Stir and fry for 2 or 3 minutes. Add scallions. Stir. Lift meat and vegetables out of pan and put into a serving dish. Mix bouillon, cornstarch, and soy sauce. Pour into frying pan and cook, stirring constantly until thick. Put noodles into center of serving dish with pork and vegetables around them. Pour sauce over meat and vegetables and serve.

# MAUI CHOW FUN
(BRAISED NOODLES)

1 pound boneless lean pork, cut in ½-inch-square strips, marinated
1 (8-oz.) package egg noodles, cooked
2 to 3 tablespoons peanut oil
1 (8-oz.) package fresh bean sprouts, blanched*
    or 1 (16-oz.) can bean sprouts, drained
2 scallions, cut into ½-inch-long pieces
1 slice fresh ginger root, crushed
    or ½ teaspoon ground ginger
1 teaspoon sugar
3 tablespoons soy sauce
1 teaspoon sesame seeds

MARINADE:
2 tablespoons soy sauce
1 teaspoon sugar
1 teaspoon salt

*TO BLANCH:
    Cover with boiling water.
    Let stand 5 minutes. Drain.

Soak pork strips in marinade for 15 minutes. Remove. Fry in oil until brown. Add cooked noodles. Add ginger, sugar and soy sauce. Stir and fry for a few minutes. Add drained bean sprouts and scallions. Stir and cook 5 minutes. Add sesame seeds and stir. Serve with chopsticks.

# COCONUT MILK BREAD

(MOOREAN)

1 cup coconut milk (page 5), scalded and cooled
1 package dry yeast, dissolved in ¼ cup lukewarm water
1 tablespoon sugar
1 cup sifted flour
1 egg, well beaten
3 tablespoons sugar
1 teaspoon salt
4 tablespoons butter or margarine, melted
3 cups sifted flour

Put cooled coconut milk in deep mixing bowl. Dissolve yeast in lukewarm water and add 1 tablespoon sugar. Add yeast mixture to coconut milk. Add 1 cup sifted flour. Beat well. Cover with thin cloth and let rise in warm place 15 minutes. Add beaten egg, salt, sugar, melted butter and 3 cups flour. Beat well. Knead for 5 minutes. Cover and let rise until double in bulk. Divide dough in half. Put in 2 greased bread tins and let rise until double. Bake 400° for about 40 minutes.

# VANILLA EXTRACT

2 cups light rum
4 or 5 vanilla beans

Put rum in glass jar. Cut vanilla beans in half, then split down center lengthwise. Add to rum. Cover and set jar in warm, sunny place for 2 to 3 weeks.
Remove beans.

# HAWAIIAN HAUPIA
(COCONUT MILK PUDDING)

1½ cups coconut milk (page 5)
 3 tablespoons sugar
 3 tablespoons cornstarch
 ⅛ teaspoon salt

Make a paste of cornstarch, sugar, salt and ½ cup coconut milk. Put 1 cup
coconut milk in saucepan and heat to boiling point. Add paste slowly, stirring
constantly until mixture is smooth and thick. Pour out into 8-inch-square
cake pan. Cool. Chill 2 to 3 hours. Cut into 1½-inch squares and serve on
freshly-washed lemon or orange leaves. (4 servings)

# CUSTARD A LA PAPEETE

3 egg yolks, beaten
¼ cup sugar
⅛ teaspoon salt
2 cups milk

1 teaspoon vanilla extract (page 98)
Whipped cream for topping
Fresh orange slices for garnish

Add sugar and salt to beaten egg yolks and put in top of double-boiler. Scald milk in a small pan. Stir milk into egg mixture slowly. Cook over boiling water stirring constantly until mixture thickens. Cool. Add vanilla. Put into parfait glasses. Chill. Top with whipped cream. Stick a fresh orange slice on each glass edge.

# COFFEE CUSTARD

1½ cups milk
¼ cup strong coffee
    or 2 teaspoons instant coffee
2 eggs, beaten

3 tablespoons sugar
¼ teaspoon ground coriander
⅛ teaspoon salt

Add coffee or instant coffee to milk. Scald. Remove from fire. Add sugar, coriander and salt to eggs and blend. Add egg mixture to milk mixture and blend. Fill buttered custard cups 2/3 full. Set cups in pan of hot water. Bake 350° oven for 30 minutes or until set. Remove cups from water. Cool. Chill. (4 servings.)

# CHOCOLATE CUSTARD

2 cups milk, scalded
¾ cup sugar
1/3 cup sifted flour
¼ teaspoon salt
6 tablespoons cocoa
4 egg yolks
2 tablespoons butter
1 teaspoon vanilla (page 98)
Whipping cream for topping

Put sugar, flour, salt, and cocoa into a bowl and mix. Add scalded milk and mix. Pour through a sieve into a heavy saucepan. Cook, stirring constantly with a wooden spoon until thick and smooth. Remove from fire. Beat egg yolks and add slowly to hot mixture. Return to fire and continue cooking and stirring for another minute. Do not boil. Stir in butter and vanilla. Cover, cool, and serve with whipped cream on top.

# LIME LECHE FLAN
(BAKED CUSTARD)

1 cup sugar for caramelizing
8 egg yolks
3 egg whites
4 cups milk
1 cup sugar
¼ teaspoon salt
1½ teaspoons vanilla (page 98)
2 teaspoons finely grated lime rind

Put 1 cup of sugar into a heavy baking dish and put over medium heat. Stir constantly until sugar melts and turns golden. Remove pan from heat and swirl caramel around until the bottom of the pan is evenly covered. Let cool. Beat egg yolks and whites together until thick. Beat in half of the milk, then add the sugar and beat until it is dissolved. Add rest of milk, salt, vanilla, and lime rind. Pour into the caramel-coated baking dish. Set the baking dish in another larger pan filled to a one-inch depth with hot water. Bake at 325° for about an hour or until a silver knife blade inserted in the center of the custard comes out clean. Remove from oven, invert a plate over the top of the pudding dish, and reverse the pudding while it is still warm. Cut into slices as you would cake.

# BANANA PUDDING

½ cup raisins
2 tablespoons brandy
¼ cup brown sugar
2 tablespoons soft butter
6 large ripe bananas
2 tablespoons light rum
2 tablespoons flour
1 tablespoon milk
¼ cup chopped pecans
   Whipping cream
   Cinnamon and nutmeg for topping

Put raisins into small bowl, add brandy, and let soak for an hour or more. Cream sugar and butter together until light. Mash the bananas, then beat them into the creamed mixture. Add rum, flour, and milk and beat again. Drain raisins and add. Add nuts. Stir until blended. Pour into layer cake tin and bake at 375° for 45 minutes or until pudding is firm. Chill. Top with sweetened whipped cream and sprinkle with cinnamon and freshly grated nutmeg.

# COCONUT CAKE

2 cups sifted cake flour
3 teaspoons double-acting baking powder
1½ cups sugar
4 tablespoons butter
6 egg whites
½ teaspoon salt
1 cup coconut milk (page 5)
1 teaspoon vanilla extract (page 98)
1 cup fresh or canned flaked coconut
¼ cup grated fresh lime peel

Sift flour, baking powder and sugar together into deep bowl. Add butter. Cream until light. Add salt to egg whites. Beat until stiff. Add coconut milk to flour mixture and beat. Fold in egg whites. Add vanilla. Place in 2 (9-inch) cake tins or 1 rectangular baking pan. Bake 40 minutes at 350°. Cool. Frost. Sprinkle with flaked coconut and grated lime peel.

# MELANESIAN MACAROONS

3 egg whites
1 cup sugar
½ teaspoon cornstarch
¾ teaspoon vanilla extract (page 98)
1½ cups fresh or packaged flaked coconut
Sliced almonds or macadamia nuts for topping

Beat egg whites until stiff, adding sugar a few tablespoonsful at a time and beating after each addition. Add cornstarch and beat in. Add vanilla and beat in. Add coconut and fold in lightly. Drop one tablespoonful at a time on greased cookie sheets. Put two or three slices of almonds or macadamia nuts on top of each macaroon. Bake at 275° until just golden-tinted (2 dozen).

# LEMON CAKE

    Grated rind of 2 lemons
½ cup sugar
½ cup unsalted butter or margarine
2 eggs, beaten
1 scant cup cake flour
1 teaspoon baking powder

Cream butter and sugar until light and fluffy. Add lemon rind. Add beaten eggs and beat well. Sift flour and baking powder together, then add gradually to creamed mixture, beating until light. Pour batter into greased cake pan. Bake at 350° for 20 to 30 minutes or until light brown. Cool on rack.

TOPPING:
    Juice of 1 lemon
½ cup powdered sugar

Mix juice and sugar. Spread on cake top while cake is cooling.

# POUND CAKE

1 pound butter
1 pound sugar
10 egg whites, beaten stiff
10 egg yolks, beaten until lemon color
1 pound flour
½ teaspoon salt
½ teaspoon mace
2 tablespoons brandy

Cream butter and sugar, adding sugar gradually, until light and fluffy. Add egg yolks. Fold in egg whites. Sift flour, salt, and mace together and beat in. Add brandy. Beat well. Pour batter into 2 greased (9 × 5-inch) loaf pans lined with heavy waxed paper. Bake at 325° for an hour.

COCONUT POUND CAKE:
Add grated meat of half a fresh coconut to cake batter.

# FRUIT SAUCE FOR CAKE

4 tablespoons butter
2 pears, peeled, cored, sliced
1 cup strawberries, washed
1 banana, sliced
1 cup apricot pulp (made from canned apricots)
¼ cup rum, heated
    Slices of pound cake

Melt butter in chafing dish. Sauté pear slices, strawberries and bananas until fruit is hot. Add apricot pulp and cook for a few minutes. Pour heated rum over the fruit. You can light it and flame it if you wish at this point. Serve immediately poured over slices of pound cake (page 106).

# MOCHA FROSTING

1½ tablespoons butter
1½ cups powdered sugar
  2 tablespoons cocoa
  3 tablespoons brewed coffee
  ⅛ teaspoon salt
  1 teaspoon vanilla (page 98)

Cream butter and sugar. Add cocoa, coffee, salt, and vanilla and stir until well blended and creamy. Spread on cooled cake.

# PIE PASTRY
(FOR 2 SINGLE 9-INCH CRUSTS)

2 cups cake flour
½ teaspoon salt
1 teaspoon baking powder
6 tablespoons shortening (2 tablespoons should be butter)
¼ cup ice water

Sift flour, salt, and baking powder together into a mixing bowl. Cut the short-ening into the flour mixture with two knives or your fingertips until the mixture resembles coarse meal. Add the water one tablespoonful at a time, tossing and blending lightly until the dough will hold together enough to form a ball. Divide the ball into 2 parts, wrap them in waxed paper and chill for half an hour. Roll out the dough between two pieces of waxed paper. Line the inside of the tin and crimp edges. Prick the shell with a fork in several places. Put a circle of foil on the bottom of the shell, turn the edges of the foil up to form a cup, and spread a layer of dried beans on it to keep the pastry flat while baking. Bake 10 minutes at 450°, remove foil with beans, return to oven for a few more minutes until lightly browned.

# MACADAMIA NUT PIE CRUST

8 tablespoons butter or margarine, softened
1 cup flour
¼ cup white sugar
¼ cup brown sugar
½ cup coarsely chopped macadamia nuts


Mix butter and flour. Add sugar and nuts and mix well. Spread on bottom of buttered pie tin. Bake at 400° for 15 minutes, stirring every 5 minutes. Remove from oven. Press mixture with back of a tablespoon to form crust. Chill.

# CHOCOLATE PIE

1 cup milk, scalded
¼ cup cocoa
½ cup sugar
⅛ teaspoon salt
3½ teaspoons cornstarch
2 tablespoons milk
2 egg yolks, beaten
1½ tablespoons butter
½ teaspoon vanilla (page 98)
Whipping cream

Put milk into heavy saucepan over very low heat and bring to boiling point to scald. Mix cocoa, sugar, and salt. Dissolve cornstarch in the 2 tablespoons of milk and stir until dissolved. Add cocoa mixture to milk and stir until mixture comes to boiling point. Add cornstarch gradually, stirring constantly, and cook until quite thick. Turn down heat. Add egg yolks and stir and cook for another minute. Do not boil. Add butter and vanilla. Beat until smooth. Cool. Pour into macadamia nut crust (page 109). Top with whipped cream.

# MACADAMIA NUT CREAM PIE

   1 cup milk
   ¼ cup sugar
   3 tablespoons chopped macadamia nuts
     Pinch of salt
   ½ teaspoon vanilla
1/3 cup milk
   1 egg
 1½ tablespoons cornstarch
   1 egg white
   ¼ cup sugar
   ¼ cup minced macadamia nuts
     Whipping cream

Put milk, sugar, nuts, salt, and vanilla into a double boiler and boil for 5 minutes. Mix the 1/3 cup milk, egg, and cornstarch thoroughly and add slowly to the boiling mixture. Stir and cook until thick. Beat egg white and sugar until stiff and fold carefully into the thickened custard. Pour custard into baked, cooled 9-inch pie shell (page 108). When cool, top with whipped cream and sprinkle with the ¼ cup macadamia nuts.

# TAHITIAN PIES
(BORA BORA)

3 cups sifted flour
1 teaspoon salt
3 teaspoons double-acting baking powder
8 tablespoons margarine
4 tablespoons butter
½ cup ice water
2 tablespoons coconut milk (page 5) mixed with 1 egg, for
    glazing (optional).

Put sifted flour in deep bowl. Re-sift with salt and baking powder. Add margarine and butter by cutting in bits of both with 2 knife blades, or blend with pastry blender or fingertips until mixture resembles coarse meal. Add ice water one tablespoonful at a time while blending with fork or pastry blender until dough holds together. Form into ball by pressing down lightly with hands. Divide dough into 8 balls. Chill ½ hour. Put balls, one at a time, on floured pastry board or cloth and roll to ⅛-inch thickness. Lay a 6-inch-wide saucer on dough and run a sharp knife blade around edge to form circle of dough. Each ball should make 2 circles. Makes 16 crusts. (Balls of dough can be wrapped in waxed paper and kept in refrigerator for several days.)

Add filling. Fold over into half-circles. Crimp edges together securely by pressing with fork tines. Place on ungreased cookie sheets or in shallow baking pans. Glaze with milk and egg mixture. Bake 15 to 20 minutes at 400° or until lightly browned.

## CREAM FILLING:
 3 egg yolks, beaten
 ½ cup sugar
 ¼ teaspoon salt
 3 tablespoons cornstarch
 2 cups milk
 1 tablespoon butter

Put egg yolks in saucepan or double-boiler top. Beat in sugar, salt and corn-starch. Heat milk to boiling in another saucepan; then add butter and stir until melted. Pour milk slowly over egg yolks while stirring. Cook and stir over low heat or boiling water until thick and smooth. Cool.

Make assorted fillings by combining 2 tablespoons cream filling with 2 or 3 tablespoons of flaked coconut, or chopped fruits such as bananas, peaches, apricots, papayas, mangoes or pineapple.

# LIME PIE

1 package (3-oz.) lime gelatin
1 cup hot water
2 teaspoons grated lime rind
½ cup lime juice
2 eggs, separated
1 (14-oz.) can sweetened condensed milk
1 baked pie crust (page 108)
Whipping cream

Dissolve gelatin in hot water in a bowl. Stir until gelatin is dissolved. Beat egg yolks until yellow, then add to jello mixture. Add milk and stir until well blended. Beat egg whites until stiff and fold in. Pour into baked pie shell. Top with whipped cream. Refrigerate 4 hours before serving.

# TONGA FRUIT PIE

1 (9-inch) baked pie crust

FILLING:
  1 cup canned diced pineapple, drained
  1 cup canned diced papaya or mango, drained
  1 apple, peeled, sliced thin
  ¼ cup white raisins
  2 tablespoons cornstarch
  ½ cup sugar
  ½ teaspoon salt
  2 egg yolks
    Juice of ½ lemon

MERINGUE:
  2 egg whites
  3 tablespoons sugar

Put pineapple, papaya, apples and raisins in saucepan. Cook 5 minutes. Mix cornstarch, sugar and salt and add to fruit mixture. Cook, stirring constantly, until thick. Beat egg yolks slightly, adding lemon juice as you beat. Add to fruit mixture and stir until eggs thicken. Pour into baked pie crust. Beat egg whites until firm, adding sugar as you beat. Spread meringue in swirls on top of filling. Bake at 325° until golden.

# PAPAYAS WITH RUM & LIME SAUCE

3 fresh papayas (allow ½ papaya per person)
1 box strawberries, washed, sliced
2 bananas, peeled, sliced

Cut papayas into halves and scoop out seeds. Fill with strawberries and bananas. Make the sauce below, cool, pour over fruit. Cover and chill before serving.

SAUCE:
2/3 cup sugar
1/3 cup water
  6 tablespoons lime juice
  ½ cup light rum

Combine sugar and water in a saucepan and bring to a boil. Turn down heat and simmer for 5 minutes. Remove from fire and cool. Add lime juice and rum.

# DRINKS

Island drinks are many and varied, ranging from non-alcoholic tropical fruit punches and iced coconut milk, through mildly alcoholic local beers and imported wines, to formidable combinations of rums and spirits. Choose drinks for feast menus from the following. Serve them island-style in large glasses with sticks of pineapple, slices of fruit and fresh flowers for decoration.

# SYRUPS

(Syrups can be made ahead of time, bottled and refrigerated until needed.)

SUGAR SYRUP:
Boil 1 cup water and 2 cups sugar for 5 minutes. Cool.

COCONUT SYRUP:
Boil 1 cup water, 2 cups sugar and ½ cup flaked coconut for 5 minutes. Cool. Strain.

# MAI TAI

1 ounce light rum
1 ounce dark rum
½ ounce cointreau
½ ounce lime juice
½ cup unsweetened pineapple juice
½ cup cracked ice

Combine ingredients in blender. Blend 15 seconds. Pour into (14-oz.) glass. Top with mint leaves.

# CHI CHI

¾ cup unsweetened pineapple juice
2 tablespoons coconut syrup (page 118)
2 ounces vodka

Combine all ingredients in shaker. Shake well and pour over crushed ice in (14-oz.) glass.

# SCORPION

2 ounces light rum
1 ounce brandy
3 tablespoons fresh orange juice
2 tablespoons fresh lemon juice
    Dash of almond extract
1 cup crushed ice

Combine all ingredients in blender. Blend 30 seconds. Pour into (14-oz.) glass.

# TAHITI PUNCH

1 ounce light rum
1 ounce dark rum
½ ounce dry white wine
1 teaspoon pineapple juice
½ teaspoon sugar syrup (page 118)
1 slice each of fresh lemon, lime and orange

Mix all ingredients in shaker. Shake well. Pour over ice into tall glass.

# TONGA PUNCH

2 ounces light rum
½ ounce curaçao
3 tablespoons orange juice

2 tablespoons lemon juice
Juice of ½ lime

Combine all ingredients in blender. Blend 15 seconds. Pour over ice into tall glass.

# FIJI FIZZ

2 ounces gin
Juice of ½ lime
1½ teaspoons sugar

Dash of Angostura bitters
8 ounces soda water

Mix all ingredients except soda in shaker. Shake well. Pour over ice into (14-oz.) glass. Fill glass with soda water.

# KAHLUA

2 cups sugar
½ cup instant coffee
2 tablespoons cocoa

1 cup boiling water
1 cup blended whiskey
½ teaspoon vanilla

Mix sugar, coffee and cocoa together. Add boiling water. Mix well. Cool. Skim foam. Add whiskey and vanilla. Mix.

# PUNCH BOWL PUNCHES

KAHALA PUNCH
- 1 bottle (one fifth or one quart) light rum
- 1 cup lemon juice
- 1 cup lime juice
- 1 cup pineapple juice
- 1 quart orange juice

Mix ingredients. Pour into punch bowl over chunks of ice and stir well. Float mint leaves on top. (For 12.)

TEA PUNCH (non-alcoholic)
- 4 tablespoons black tea leaves
- 1 cup boiling water
- 2 lemons
- 1 cup sugar
- 4 cups cold water
- ½ teaspoon vanilla extract
- 2 dashes almond extract
- 1 (28-oz.) bottle ginger ale
- 1 (8½-oz.) can crushed pineapple

Pour 1 cup boiling water over tea leaves. Cover and steep 10 minutes. Wash lemons. Cut in half. Extract juice. Scrape pulp out of rinds and slice rinds in very thin slices. Put lemon rinds, juice, cold water and sugar in saucepan and heat, stirring until sugar is dissolved. Strain tea and add. Cool. Add vanilla and almond extracts. Chill. When ready to serve pour into punch bowl over chunks of ice. Add ginger ale and pineapple. (For 12.)